A Child's E

Sisters of Notre Dame of Chardon, Ohio

by
Sister Mary Kathleen Glavich, S.N.D.

This book belongs to

_____

LOYOLAPRESS.
CHICAGO

Nihil Obstat: The Reverend Ronald H. Bojarski, Ph.D.
                  Censor Deputatus
Imprimatur: The Most Reverend Anthony M. Pilla, D.D., M.A.
                  Bishop of Cleveland
Given at Cleveland, Ohio, on 20 February 1990.

Glavich, Mary Kathleen.
    A child's Bible/Mary Kathleen Glavich; Sisters of Notre Dame of Chardon, Ohio.
        p. cm.
    Summary: A simple retelling of twelve stories from the Old and New Testaments.
    ISBN 0-8294-0718-9
    1. Bible stories, English. [1. Bible stories.] I. Sisters of Notre Dame of Chardon, Ohio. II Title.
BS551.2.G535   1990   90-90-26030
220.9'505—dc20   CIP
                                                             AC

Acknowledgments
The author would like to acknowledge and thank the following people: those who supported the project, especially Sister Mary Joell Overman, S.N.D.; Sister Rita Mary Harwood, S.N.D.; and Sister Mary Nathan, S.N.D.; Marilyn Jones and Elaine Reardon, who graciously read the manuscript; those who worked on different stages of the production, especially Sister Mary Julie Boehnlein, S.N.D.; Sister Mary Beth Gray, S.N.D.; Sister Mary Andrew Miller, S.N.D.; and Sister Mary St. Jude Weisensell, S.N.D.
Interior and cover art by Lydia Halverson.

ISBN 13: 978-0-8294-2518-5   ISBN 10: 0-8294-2518-7

07 08 09 10 11 12 13 14 15 16 Web 10 9 8 7 6 5 4 3 2 1

LOYOLAPRESS.
3441 N. ASHLAND AVENUE
CHICAGO, ILLINOIS 60657
(800) 621-1008
www.LoyolaPress.org

Contents

Noah, the Flood, and the Rainbow

Based on Genesis 6:5-9;17

Once, long ago, most of the people in the world were very wicked. Only Noah and his family lived the way God had asked. God decided to make the world over.

God told Noah to build an ark, an enormous boat. God said, "I am about to flood the earth. Go into the ark with your family. Take with you two of every animal, one male and one female. Put enough food in the ark for all."

1

Noah did as God told him. He built the ark and put into it two of every animal. Then he and his family went into the ark. It began to rain. It poured for forty days and forty nights. The whole earth was flooded, but the ark floated on the water. Everything died except Noah, his family, and the animals in the ark. Suddenly the rains stopped. Then God sent wind to dry up the water.

One day Noah sent out a dove. It came back with an olive leaf. So Noah knew the water was going down.

Finally, the earth was dry. Noah, his family, and every animal left the ark. Noah thanked God for saving them.

God loved Noah. He loved all the creatures he had made. God blessed them and promised Noah that he would never flood the earth again.

3

Then God gave us a sign of his promise and his great love. He put a rainbow in the sky.

❖ Tell Jesus that you love him, too.

4

Joseph and His Brothers

Based on Genesis 37:3–46:34

Jacob had twelve sons. His favorite son was Joseph, one of the youngest. Jacob made Joseph a beautiful, long coat. Joseph's brothers were jealous. They wouldn't even talk to him.

6

One day the brothers were taking care of the sheep. Joseph stayed at home. Jacob sent Joseph to see if his brothers were all right. When Joseph came to the brothers, they took away his coat. Then they threw him into an empty well.

As the brothers ate, a group of people traveling to Egypt was passing by. One brother, Judah, said, "Why kill Joseph? Let's sell him to these people." So Joseph's brothers sold him for twenty silver coins.

The brothers dipped Joseph's coat in goat's blood and sent it to Jacob. When Jacob saw the coat, he thought, "A wild animal has killed my son." He cried for many days.

Meanwhile, the people who bought Joseph took him to Egypt. Joseph worked hard there. He always did what was right. Soon the king of Egypt put Joseph in charge of the whole country.

God let Joseph know that a time was coming when there would be no food. Joseph had the people of Egypt store grain. Then when the rest of the world was hungry, Egypt had plenty to eat. People from other countries came to Joseph for food.

Joseph's brothers traveled to Egypt to get food, too. They didn't recognize Joseph. He knew who they were, though. Joseph did not scold his brothers or put them in jail. Instead he gave them food to take home.

Finally Joseph said to them, "I am Joseph. Is my father well?" Then he invited his brothers and his father to move to Egypt. And they did.

Jacob was very happy to see that Joseph was alive. Jacob, Joseph, Joseph's brothers, and their families lived together in Egypt for many years.

❖ Ask Jesus to help you to forgive others as Joseph did.

8

A Strange Night for Samuel

Based on 1 Samuel 3:1–18

The boy Samuel lived in the Temple of the Lord. Eli, the priest, took care of him. One night Samuel was asleep in the Temple. God called, "Samuel. Samuel."

Samuel woke up and ran to Eli. He said, "Here I am. You called me."

Eli said, "I did not call you. Go back to sleep." Samuel went back to sleep.

Again God called, "Samuel. Samuel." Again Samuel got up and went to Eli. He said, "Here I am. You called me."

But Eli said, "I did not call you, my son. Go back to sleep." Samuel did.

For the third time God called, "Samuel. Samuel."

Samuel went to Eli and said, "Here I am. You called me."

Then Eli knew that God was calling Samuel. He said to the boy, "Go to sleep. If you are called again, answer, 'Speak, Lord, for your servant is listening.'"

Samuel went back to sleep. God called again, "Samuel. Samuel." This time Samuel answered, "Speak, Lord, for your servant is listening."

God gave Samuel a message for Eli that night. Samuel grew up to be a holy man. He gave many people messages from God.

❖   Ask Jesus to give you a listening heart.

David, the Shepherd-King
Based on 1 Samuel 16:1–13

The king of Israel did not obey God. God said to Samuel, "Go to Jesse in Bethlehem. I have chosen one of his sons to be the new king. I will point out to you the one I have chosen. Anoint him with oil."

When Samuel came to Bethlehem, he met Jesse. He saw one of Jesse's sons who was very tall. He thought, "This must be the new king."

But God said, "No. I don't choose by looks but by what's in the heart."

So Jesse brought a second son to Samuel. But Samuel said, "No. God has not chosen him."

Jesse brought five more sons to Samuel. Each time Samuel said, "No. This is not the one."

Then Samuel asked Jesse, "Do you have any more sons?" Jesse answered, "There is still the youngest boy who is tending the sheep."

Samuel said, "Send for him."

When young David came, God said to Samuel, "Anoint him. This is the one."

So God, through Samuel, made David king. David grew up to be the greatest king Israel ever had.

❖ Ask Jesus to help you make good choices.

12

13

Mary's Visit

Based on Luke 1:36–56

The angel Gabriel asked Mary to be the Mother of Jesus. Mary said yes. The angel said that Mary's cousin Elizabeth was going to have a baby too.

Elizabeth was old. Mary knew it would be hard for her to take care of the house, to get water from the well, and to cook.

Mary thought, "Elizabeth needs help. I will go to her." Mary showed her love for Elizabeth and for God.

Mary traveled many miles to Elizabeth's house. She walked or rode a donkey.

When Mary arrived, Elizabeth was surprised. She hugged Mary and greeted her as the Mother of God. Even the baby inside Elizabeth jumped for joy.

Mary helped Elizabeth for a few months. Then she went back home to prepare for Jesus to be born.

❖ Ask Jesus to help you be kind like his mother, Mary.

16

The Thankful Man

Based on Luke 17:11–19

One day Jesus met ten sick men. They had a terrible disease.

The ten sick men shouted to Jesus, "Jesus, have pity on us!"

Jesus said to them, "Go to the priests. They will see that you are cured."

As the ten men walked along on their way to the priests, they were healed. Their faces were healed. Their arms were healed. Their legs were healed.

One man ran back to Jesus. He knelt before Jesus and said, "Thank you." He praised God for curing him.

Jesus was happy to see this man. But he asked, "Weren't ten men healed? Where are the other nine?"

Only one man had thought to say thank you.

❖   Thank Jesus for something he has done for you.

Jesus' Wonderful Picnic

Based on John 6:1–15

One day Jesus was teaching a huge crowd of people. His best friends, who were called disciples, came to him. They said, "It's very late. Let the people go so they can buy something to eat." Jesus told his disciples "You give them food." The men knew they could never buy enough food for all the people.

The disciple Andrew said, "There is a boy here who has five loaves of bread and two fish. But that is not enough."

Jesus took the boy's bread. He thanked God for it and passed it out. He passed out the fish, too. The people had as much as they wanted.

When the disciples collected the leftovers, they filled twelve baskets!

Jesus had power to feed all the hungry people.

❖ Thank Jesus for giving us food, especially himself in Communion.

19

The Girl Who Came Back to Life

Based on Luke 8:40–56

One day a large crowd was around Jesus. A man named Jairus came to him. He knelt at Jesus' feet and begged, "Please come to my house. My only daughter—my little girl—is dying."

Right away, Jesus went with Jairus. On the way, someone from Jairus's house met them. He said to Jairus, "Your daughter is dead. Jesus doesn't have to come."

But Jesus said, "Do not be afraid. Trust me."

When they came to the house, everyone was crying for the girl. Jesus said, "Do not cry. The girl is not dead. She is sleeping." The people laughed at Jesus.

Jesus entered the house. He went to the girl and took her hand. He said, "Little girl, arise." The girl began to breathe again. She got up.

Her mother and father were surprised and happy. Jesus said to them, "Give her something to eat."

❖ Tell Jesus that you trust him.

The Man by the Pool

Based on John 5:1–18

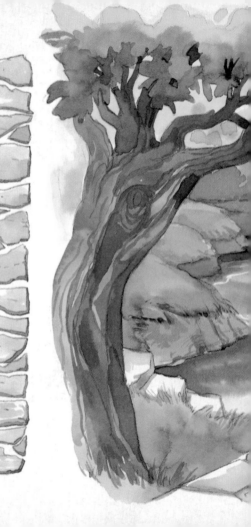

In Jerusalem there was a pool with healing water. When the water moved, the first sick person to go into the pool was cured. Many blind people, deaf people, crippled people, and sick people waited at the pool. They hoped they would be healed.

One day Jesus came to the pool. He saw a man lying there on a mat. Jesus knew this man had been sick for thirty-eight years.

Jesus asked the man, "Do you want to be well?"

The man said, "I have no one to put me into the water. Someone always gets there before I do."

Jesus said to the man, "Rise, take up your mat, and walk."

Just like that, the man was healed. He stood up, picked up his mat, and walked away.

❖ Ask Jesus for something that you or someone in your family needs.

22

23

Zaccheus Sees

Based on Luke 19:1–10

In the town of Jericho lived a tax collector named Zacchaeus. No one liked him. As he collected taxes, he cheated people and kept some of the money for himself.

One day Jesus was passing through Jericho. Everyone wanted to see him. So did Zacchaeus, but Zacchaeus was very short. When he looked for Jesus coming down the road, he couldn't see over the crowd.

Zacchaeus was smart. He ran ahead and climbed a sycamore tree. From there he could see everything. He saw Jesus.

Suddenly Jesus stopped on the road, right under the sycamore tree! He looked up and saw Zacchaeus. Jesus knew that Zacchaeus had sinned, but he loved Zacchaeus. He said, "Zacchaeus, come down. I will stay at your house today."

Zacchaeus came down the tree quickly. He was happy that Jesus had chosen him, but the people were upset. They said, "Jesus is going to the house of a sinner."

24

Zacchaeus was sorry for hurting others. He promised to
pay back even more money than he had taken. Jesus
forgave him, and Zacchaeus became a better person.

❖ Ask Jesus to forgive you for something you did wrong.

Breakfast on the Beach

Based on John 21:1–14

Most of Jesus' best friends were fishermen. Once they were out fishing all night long but caught nothing. When the sun came up, they were tired and unhappy. Jesus was standing on the shore. He called out to them, "Throw your net over the right side of the boat and you will find something."

The men did as Jesus said. So many fish swam into the net that the fishermen couldn't pull it into the boat. They had to drag it to shore behind the boat. With Jesus' help they had caught one hundred fifty-three large fish.

When the friends of Jesus arrived on the shore, they saw that Jesus had a fire going and was cooking fish and bread. He had made breakfast for them. Jesus always did kind and loving things for others.

❖ Ask Jesus to show you ways to help others.

The Buried Treasure

Based on Matthew 13:44

Once a man was digging in a field. He dug and dug and dug. All of a sudden—*klunk!* His spade hit something. It was not a rock. What was it? The man dug some more.

It was a treasure buried in the ground!

The man was excited and full of joy. He knew that if he owned the field, the treasure would belong to him. He buried the treasure again. Then he ran off to buy the field.

But he needed money. To get the money, the man sold everything he owned. He sold his house, his animals, and his furniture. Then he bought the field. The treasure was his!

❖ Ask Jesus to help you to want heaven as much as the man wanted the treasure.